STAR BIOGRAPHIES

The Jonas Brothers

by Jennifer M. Besel

CAPSTONE PRESS
a capstone imprint

Snap Books are published by Capstone Press,
151 Good Counsel Drive, P.O. Box 669, Mankato, Minnesota 56002.
www.capstonepress.com

092009
005618CGS10

Library of Congress Cataloging-in-Publication Data
Besel, Jennifer M.
    The Jonas Brothers / by Jennifer M. Besel.
    p. cm. — (Snap books. Star biographies)
    Includes bibliographical references and index.
    Summary: "Describes the life and career of the Jonas Brothers" — Provided by publisher.
    ISBN 978-1-4296-4011-4 (library binding)
    1. Jonas Brothers — Juvenile literature. 2. Rock musicians — United States — Biography — Juvenile literature.
I. Title.
ML3930.J62B47 2010
782.42164092'2 — dc22

                                                            2009026640

Editor: Kathryn Clay
Designer: Juliette Peters
Media Researcher: Marcie Spence
Production Specialist: Laura Manthe

Photo Credits:
AdMedia/Russ Elliot, 15
AP Images for Nickelodeon/Evans Ward, 11; Tammie Arroyo, cover
CORBIS/Jon McKee/Retna Ltd., 13; Mario Anzuoni/Reuters, 7
Getty Images for MTV/Frank Micelotta, 20
Getty Images Inc./Eric Charbonneau/Le Studio/Wireimage, 29; Gilbert Carrasquillo/FilmMagic, 28; Jeff Kravitz/
        FilmMagic, 23 (bottom); Jordan Strauss/WireImage, 10; Kevin Mazur/WireImage, 17
Globe Photos/Henry McGee, 25
Newscom, 5; ÂJuan Soliz, PacificCoastNews, 23 (top); Danielle P. Richards/Bergen Record, 9; Pedro Andrade/
        Kevin Perkins, 21; PNP/WENN, 24; Splash News and Pictures, 27
Rex USA/c.W. Disney/Everett, 16
Walt Disney Pictures/The Kobal Collection, 19

Essential content terms are **bold** and are defined at the bottom of the page where they first appear.

Table of Contents

A Breakthrough Night

Dressed in designer suits, Kevin, Joe, and Nick Jonas strutted down the red carpet. In front of the Nokia Theatre in Los Angeles, hundreds of fans screamed for their idols. The brothers were at the 2008 American Music Awards. They were **nominees** for the Breakthrough Artist of the Year award.

The show was packed with star-studded performances, including the Jonas Brothers. The brothers took the stage to perform their hit song "Tonight." Between performances, presenters handed out the awards. When Ashley Tisdale walked on stage, it was time to learn if the brothers had won.

The Jonas Brothers nervously waited for the announcement. The band's competition included Paramore, Colbie Caillat, Flo Rida, and The-Dream. Fans determined the winner by texting in their votes. When Ashley announced that the Jonas Brothers had won, the brothers broke into smiles. They had just won their first major award.

nominee — someone who is to be considered for an award or honor

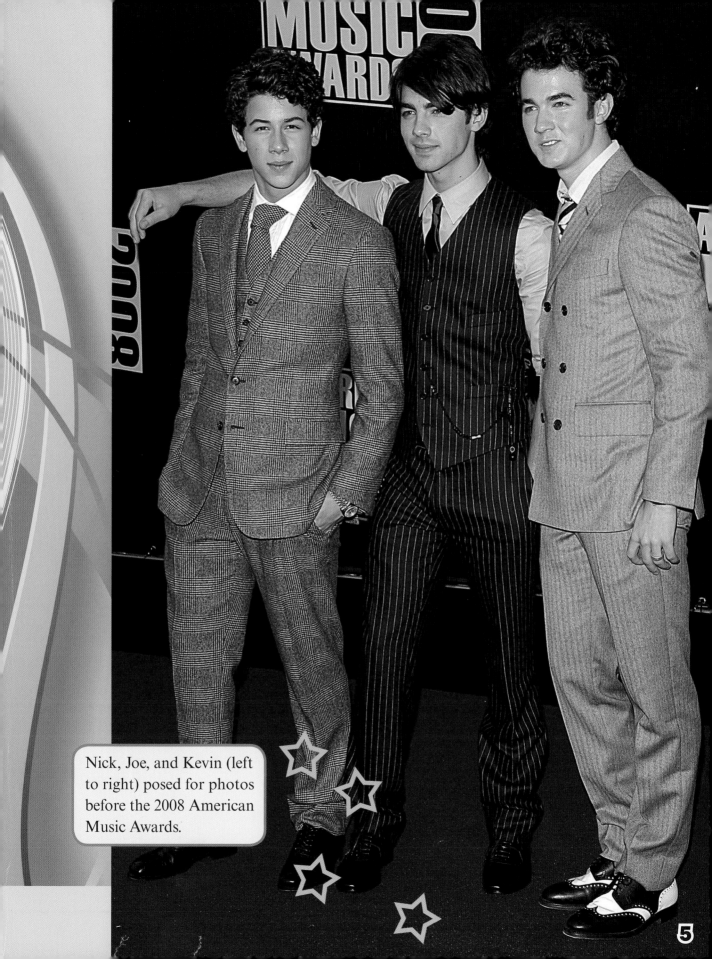

Nick, Joe, and Kevin (left to right) posed for photos before the 2008 American Music Awards.

In their acceptance speech, the brothers thanked their amazing fans. But that's not all they did to show their appreciation. Kevin, Joe, and Nick also scheduled a free concert to celebrate their nomination. They promoted the concert on the radio and on their MySpace page.

With only a day's notice, a thousand fans lined up outside the House of Blues in Los Angeles. The brothers delighted audience members with a three-hour show. Surprise guests Jordin Sparks, Demi Lovato, Jesse McCartney, and Dan Aykroyd joined the brothers on stage.

At the end of the concert, Kevin, Joe, and Nick thanked their fans again. The brothers knew they wouldn't be superstars without the support of their fans. The packed concert showed that they had come a long way from practicing in the family basement.

"We wake up every morning excited because we get to do what we love."
— Kevin in an interview with *People* magazine.

In 2008, the Jonas Brothers accepted the Breakthrough Artist of the Year Award at the American Music Awards.

A Family Foundation

The Jonas Brothers isn't just a band name. Kevin, Joe, and Nick really are brothers. Their parents, Kevin Sr. and Denise, have always made sure that family comes first. When the brothers were younger, Kevin Sr. traveled the country as a minister and songwriter. The family went with him, often spending travel time reading and singing together.

Meet the Brothers

Paul Kevin Jonas II, known as Kevin, was born in Teaneck, New Jersey, on November 5, 1987. One day when he was home sick, he found a beginning guitar book. Kevin picked up a guitar and started teaching himself to play. From that moment on, he loved to play the guitar.

Kevin was just two years old when he became a big brother. On August 15, 1989, Joseph Adam Jonas was born in Casa Grande, Arizona. Joe was quiet and calm as a young boy. As he grew up, he came out of his shy shell. At one time, Joe even dreamed of being a comedian.

The Jonas family has always been close. The family, shown here in 2000, includes Kevin Sr., Frankie, Nick, Denise, Kevin, and Joe (left to right).

Frankie (front) joined his brothers at the premiere of *Jonas Brothers: The 3D Concert Experience*.

The family was living in Dallas, Texas, when Nicholas Jerry Jonas was born on September 16, 1992. Nick has been singing and performing since he was a young boy. Born with **perfect pitch**, Nick amused himself by singing and making music. He also learned to play piano and drums. His passion for music eventually led to the Jonas Brothers' success.

perfect pitch — making no mistakes in the highness or lowness of musical sounds

Bonus Jonas

Frankie is the youngest brother in the Jonas family. Born on September 28, 2000, Frankie also has music in his blood. While he is too young to jam with his brothers, fans still have a special love for the young Jonas. He's even earned the nickname "Bonus Jonas." His older brothers hope Frankie will join them on stage someday.

Frankie attended the 2009 Nickelodeon Kids' Choice Awards.

Discovered!

In 1996, the Jonas family moved to Wyckoff, New Jersey. There Kevin, Joe, and Nick attended Eastern Christian School. They put on plays in their home, showing off their singing and performing skills.

While getting a haircut one day, 6-year-old Nick started singing. A woman heard Nick and told his mother to take him to a talent **agent**. Nick, Joe, and Kevin all auditioned and were offered contracts. The brothers appeared in commercials for LEGOs, Clorox, and Burger King. Then Nick landed roles in Broadway plays. He performed in *Beauty and the Beast*, *Annie Get Your Gun*, and *Les Misérables*.

As Nick's career started to bloom, Joe became more interested in music. He joined the Broadway fun by singing in the opera *La Bohéme*. He also landed roles in *The Velveteen Rabbit* and *Oliver*. Kevin practiced guitar and hoped to join a band in New York City. In their spare time, the brothers hung out in their basement and wrote music together.

agent — someone who helps actors find work

A Life-Changing Event

In November 2005, Nick received news that changed his life forever. For months, he had been losing weight and was constantly thirsty. He felt like something was wrong, but he had no idea what it was.

Finally Nick went to see a doctor. As soon as the doctor heard his symptoms, she rushed him to the hospital. At the age of 13, Nick was told he had Type 1 **diabetes**. With diabetes, the **pancreas** doesn't make the insulin needed to change sugar into energy.

There is no cure for diabetes, so Nick carefully manages his condition. He wears a pump that gives him insulin through a permanent tube. He also tests his blood up to 12 times a day to check his sugar levels. It's not fun, but Nick doesn't let it get him down.

Nick was diagnosed with Type 1 diabetes when he was 13 years old.

diabetes — a disease in which there is too much sugar in the blood

pancreas — an organ near the stomach that makes insulin

CHAPTER 3

Singing Sensations

Today Kevin, Joe, and Nick draw screaming fans everywhere they go. But this wasn't always the case. For a while, it seemed like the band didn't have a fan in the world.

In 2004, Columbia Records signed Nick as a Christian singer. But Nick's CD didn't sell well, and Columbia Records considered dropping him. Luckily, someone at Columbia believed that Nick could be a star. About the same time, Kevin, Joe, and Nick were ready to share the songs they had written in their basement. The boys played "Please Be Mine" for the company's executives. They liked the song, and all three brothers signed a recording contract. They were now a band with a record label.

"We kind of always grew up into music and making music with my dad."
— Joe in an interview with the *Houston Chronicle*.

Nick, Kevin, and Joe (left to right) attended the 2006 Teen Choice Awards.

In August 2006, the Jonas Brothers band released its first CD, *It's About Time*. The album didn't do well. Only 65,000 CDs were sold. But the band's manager, Johnny Wright, wasn't giving up.

In 2007, the Jonas Brothers worked with Billy Ray Cyrus (second from right) when they appeared on the *Hannah Montana* show.

The Brothers Meet Disney

Johnny convinced Columbia Records to end the band's contract. Then he signed the Jonas Brothers with Hollywood Records. With this new deal, the brothers hit the big time. That's because the Disney Corporation owns Hollywood Records. The brothers would now be featured on Disney Radio and on the Disney Channel.

With Disney's backing, things started to roll for the Jonas Brothers. In August 2007, the band released its second album, *Jonas Brothers*. Days later, the band performed during the *Hannah Montana* show. After that performance, the brothers' popularity exploded. Their album hit number 5 on the *Billboard Hot 200* chart. Fans scooped up more than 1 million copies of the CD, and the brothers raked in $12 million.

Rockin' on the Road

After the success of the band's second album, fans were screaming for more. The brothers got to work writing songs for their third album. Because they were on tour with Miley Cyrus, there wasn't time to get into a recording studio. Instead, the brothers came up with an idea. Hollywood Records gave the band a bus that had been turned into a recording studio. While rolling down the highway, Kevin, Joe, and Nick recorded all the songs for their new album. They recorded everything from vocals to drums. By the time the tour was over, their third album, *A Little Bit Longer*, was ready for fans.

Nick, Kevin, and Joe, performed with Miley Cyrus (third from left) during her Best of Both Worlds tour.

JoBro Mania

More than Music

The Jonas Brothers quickly became more than just singing sensations. In 2008, the brothers starred in the Disney Channel movie *Camp Rock*. Joe played Shane Gray, a rock star looking to repair his image. In the film, Shane falls for a girl named Mitchie Torres, played by Demi Lovato. Kevin and Nick played smaller roles in the film.

Next stop for the brothers was reality TV. *Jonas Brothers: Living the Dream* captured the day-to-day life of the Jonas family. Fans watched the guys do everything from eat breakfast to perform on stage. The show aired on the Disney Channel from May 2008 to September 2008.

In February 2009, *Jonas Brothers: The 3D Concert Experience* was released. The movie featured clips of the band's Burning Up tour. It also included behind-the-scenes action and guest performances from Taylor Swift and Demi Lovato. Also in 2009, the brothers had small roles in the movie *Night at the Museum: Battle of the Smithsonian*. Kevin, Joe, and Nick played singing cherubs.

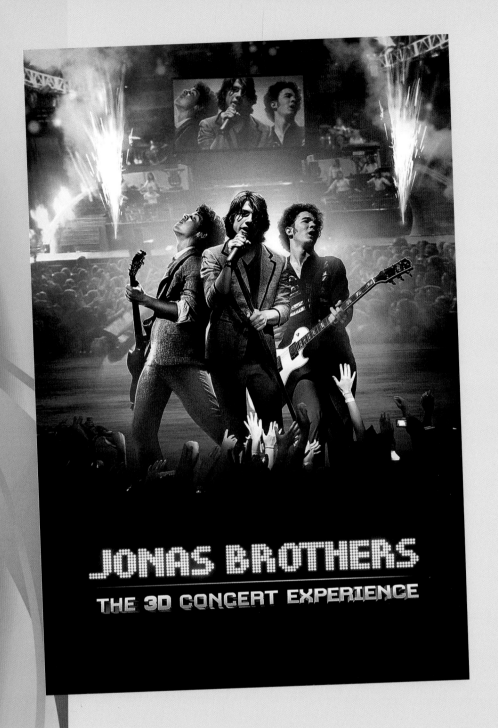

A new TV show starring the brothers debuted on the Disney Channel in May 2009. On the show *JONAS*, Kevin, Joe, and Nick play rock stars dealing with the everyday problems of fame. Even younger brother Frankie makes occasional appearances on the show.

After the success of their second album, the brothers' lives changed a lot. The family moved to Los Angeles. Screaming fans showed up wherever the guys went. Paparazzi followed their every move. The guys were also getting used to their million-dollar paychecks.

But one thing that has never changed is their strong family bond. The brothers still find time to hang out or play ball together. And when they go on tour, their parents travel with them. In fact, their dad is their co-manager.

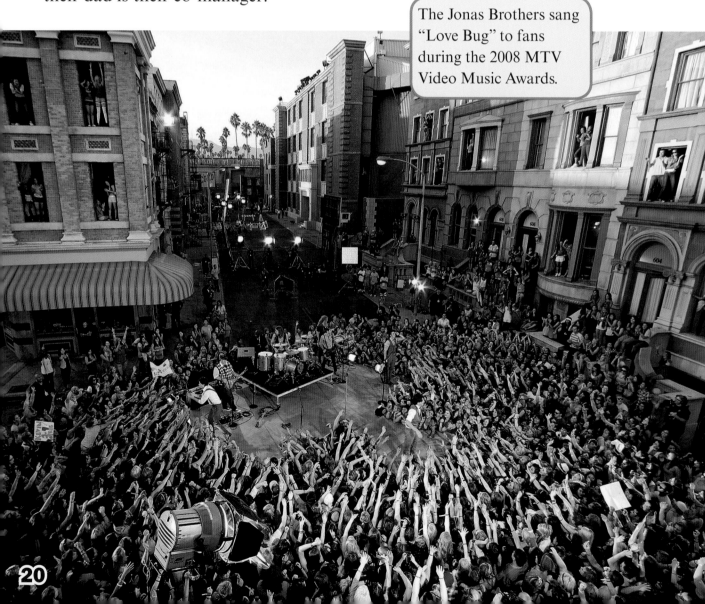

The Jonas Brothers sang "Love Bug" to fans during the 2008 MTV Video Music Awards.

Nick enjoys walking his golden retriever, Elvis.

Everyday Lives

Being megastars doesn't leave much time for relaxation. Kevin, Joe, and Nick spend their days shooting music videos and TV shows, meeting fans, and signing autographs. Other days are spent reading fan mail or recording their latest hit song.

Even with their demanding schedules, the brothers find time to be themselves. For his 16th birthday, Nick got a golden retriever he named Elvis. Kevin enjoys rolling down the road in his hybrid car. And Joe loves the motorcycle and sidecar he got for his 19th birthday.

In the Spotlight

Fans cannot get enough of Kevin, Joe, and Nick. They watch TV interviews and read magazine articles about them. Fans chat online about the brothers' sleek fashions and trendy hairstyles. They even share romance rumors.

All that attention makes it hard to keep their personal lives private. While the guys try not to talk about their relationships, word spreads quickly. Headlines shouted news about Joe's breakups with Taylor Swift and Camilla Belle. Kevin's proposal to Danielle Deleasa and Nick's relationship with Miley are also popular subjects with the **media**. The attention can be hard for the guys to deal with at times. But overall, the trio loves the spotlight.

"I think we've always tried to live our lives to some standards. The good thing is that we have each other."
— Nick in an interview with *Rolling Stone* magazine.

media — communication forms that send out messages to groups of people

Kevin proposed to girlfriend Danielle Deleasa (right) on July 1, 2009.

Joe's relationship with Taylor Swift (left) was a popular topic for fans and the media.

Giving Back

Between concerts, recording sessions, and film shoots, these guys still find time to give back. The brothers started Change for the Children Foundation as a way to inspire kids to help others. The foundation's first project was called "You Decide. You Donate." Fans donated money to support five charities. The brothers matched the donations with their own money, up to $10,000 per charity.

D-Vision is another important part of the foundation. The D-Vision program helps to raise money for diabetes research. Nick hopes his work will help researchers find a cure for diabetes.

The Jonas brothers donate part of their income to charity.

Date August 6, 2008

Bayer HealthCare
Diabetes Care

$100,000

Pay To The Order Of CHANGE FOR THE CHILDREN FOUNDATION

One Hundred Thousand DOLLARS

Bayer Diabetes Care

simplewins

Memo Thank You Nick!

Teaming Up for Diabetes Awareness

To help find a cure for diabetes, Nick teamed up with a big name in health care. Bayer is a company that makes medicine. Together Nick and Bayer are sharing information about diabetes. Through the program "Nick's Simple Wins," Nick has become a spokesperson for managing diabetes.

In 2008, Nick designed dog tags to help raise money for the cause. People can buy a dog tag and show their support for diabetes research. Each tag says, "a little bit longer and I'll be fine." This phrase isn't just a motto. It's part of a song Nick wrote about dealing with the condition. The song "A Little Bit Longer" has become a theme song for diabetes awareness. It's also the name of the brothers' third album.

Having It All

Kevin, Joe, and Nick have taken the music scene by storm. And the critics are starting to take notice. At the 2009 Grammy Awards, the band was nominated for Best New Artist. They also got a nod for the 2008 MTV Video Music Awards' Video of the Year. Though they didn't win either award, they do have their fair share of trophies.

At the 2008 Teen Choice Awards, the Jonas Brothers won five categories. Their ballad "When You Look Me in the Eyes" won for Best Single and Best Love Song. They also won awards for Best Breakout Group, Male Hottie, and Male Fashion Icon.

In 2008 and 2009, they won Favorite Music Group at the Nickelodeon Kids' Choice Awards. And of course, they had the Breakthrough Artist win at the 2008 American Music Awards.

Kevin, Joe, and Nick (left to right) dressed up in colorful outfits for the 2008 Kids' Choice Awards.

What's Next

The Jonas Brothers already have a huge list of accomplishments, but they aren't done yet. In November 2008, Kevin, Nick, and Joe released their first book, *Burning Up: On Tour with the Jonas Brothers*. Written by the brothers, the book gives fans an inside look into their lives. Their fourth album, *Lines, Vines and Trying Times*, came out in June 2009, and features the hit song "Paranoid."

And if that wasn't enough, another full-length film is in the works. Nick, Joe, Kevin, and Frankie put their acting skills to the test in the movie *Walter the Farting Dog*. In the movie, the brothers play musicians who take care of their sick aunt's gassy pooch.

In their book *Burning Up: On Tour with the Jonas Brothers*, the brothers wrote about life on the road.

The Jonas Brothers made a surprise appearance at the El Capitan Theatre in Hollywood on the opening night of *Jonas Brothers: The 3D Concert Experience*.

Right now, the sky is the limit for these young heartthrobs. They have talked about future movies, albums, and tours. They have even talked about attending the Berklee College of Music one day. No matter what the future holds, the Jonas brothers are sure to do it with style.

Glossary

agent (AY-juhnt) — someone who helps actors find work

album (AL-buhm) — a collection of music recorded on a CD, tape, or record

critic (KRIT-ik) — someone whose job is to review a CD, book, or movie

debut (DAY-byoo) — a first public appearance

diabetes (dye-uh-BEE-tuhss) — a disease in which there is too much sugar in the blood

media (MEE-dee-uh) — TV, radio, newspapers, and other communication forms that send out messages to large groups of people

nominee (nom-uh-NEE) — someone who is to be considered for an award or an honor

pancreas (PAN-kree-uhss) — an organ near the stomach that makes insulin

paparazzi (pah-puh-RAHT-see) — aggressive photographers who take pictures of celebrities for sale to magazines or newspapers

perfect pitch (PUR-fikt PICH) — making no mistakes in the highness or lowness of musical sounds

Read More

Johns, Michael-Anne. *Just Jonas: The Jonas Brothers Up Close and Personal*. New York: Scholastic, 2008.

Jonas, Joe, Kevin Jonas, and Nick Jonas. *Burning Up: On Tour with the Jonas Brothers*. New York: Disney-Hyperion Books, 2008.

Mattern, Joanne. *Jonas Brothers*. A Robbie Reader. Hockessin, Del.: Mitchell Lane, 2009.

Ryals, Lexi. *Jammin' with the Jonas Brothers: An Unauthorized Biography*. New York: Price Stern Sloan, 2008.

Internet Sites

FactHound offers a safe, fun way to find Internet sites related to this book. All of the sites on FactHound have been researched by our staff.

Here's all you do:

Visit *www.facthound.com*

FactHound will fetch the best sites for you!

Index